# Holiday

## GET-TOGETHER
## COOKBOOK

**Marilyn Tucke**

**Hearts 'N Tummies Cookbook Co.**
3544 Blakslee Street
**Wever  IA   52658**
**800-571-2665**

# DEDICATION

To my mother, Edna Elizabeth Tucker, who was the one who taught me the art of cooking and to all those after her who kept on cooking and contributing their fine recipes at our many get-togethers.

# TABLE OF CONTENTS

# BEVERAGES, APPETIZERS, SNACKS AND DIPS

# CRANBERRY CHRISTMAS TEA

1 c. cinnamon
   candies
12 whole cloves
1 qt. water
1 c. sugar

4 (1-qt.) bottles cranberry
   juice cocktail
1 small can frozen orange
   juice
1 small can frozen lemonade

Boil candies, cloves, water and sugar together until candy dissolves, stirring constantly. Add cranberry juice cocktail, orange juice, and lemonade. Add up to 3 quarts of water, starting with 1 quart, according to taste.

# FOURTH OF JULY PUNCH

3 (6-oz.) cans frozen lemonade concentrate
4 (6-oz.) cans frozen orange juice concentrate
4 (6-oz.) can frozen limeade
5 c. sugar
3 qts. chilled ginger ale

Combine all ingredients and add enough ice water to
make 2 1/2 gallons liquid.

# ICED COFFEE MOCHA

2 c. milk
1/4 c. Hershey chocolate
1 T. instant coffee

Crushed ice
Vanilla ice cream

Combine milk, Hershey chocolate, and instant coffee. Shake and pour over crushed ice. Top with scoop of ice cream.

# LISA'S WEDDING PUNCH

2 pkgs. Kool-Aid
2 (8-oz.) cans frozen orange juice
2 (8-oz.) cans frozen lemonade
2 (46-oz.) cans pineapple-grapefruit juice

Mix and let set 4 hours.  Add 2 two-liter ginger ale before serving.

# LO-CAL HAM YOGURT DIP

5 oz. cooked ham, chopped     1/4 tsp. garlic
2 c. plain low-fat yogurt     1/4 tsp. curry powder
3 small green onions, chopped     1/8 tsp. black pepper
3/4 tsp. Seasonal (seasoned salt)

Combine all ingredients. Mix well and chill. Serve with assorted fresh vegetables or may be used as a salad dressing. Makes about 2 1/2 c. (Approximately 15 calories per tablespoon.)

# DILLWEED PARTY BREAD SNACKS

Use 1 loaf party rye or pumpernickel bread.  Mix 1 pkg. cream cheese (8-oz.) with 1 pkg. dry original ranch dressing seasoning.

Spread mixture on party bread.  Sprinkle tops with dillweed (small can).

Peel and slice 2 or 3 cucumbers.  Place 1 or 2 slices on top of each slice of bread.  Keep cool until serving.

# SHRIMP DIP

1 large pkg. cream cheese - softened
1 can shrimp - drained
2 T. lemon juice
2 T. grated onion
1 T. garlic salt
2 T. Worchester sauce
1/2 to 1 c. sour cream or milk to make mixture
    thin enough to dip

Mix all ingredients together except shrimp. Stir shrimp
in last. Chill until ready to serve.

# CHEESE BALL

1 (8-oz.) pkg. cream cheese     1 T. garlic salt
1/2 (3-oz.) pkg. blue cheese     Pecans, chopped
8 oz. cheddar cheese
1/2 c. ripe olives, chopped
1/4 c. stuffed green olives, chopped
2 T. onion flakes

Mix cheeses; add olives, onion flakes and garlic salt. Chill 1 hour, roll into a ball and then in chopped pecans.

# DELICIOUS SHRIMP DIP

2 6-oz. cans small shrimp, drained
1 8-oz. pkg. cream cheese
1/2 small onion, grated
2 T. ketchup
1 T. horseradish
Salt and pepper to taste

Combine all ingredients and stir together. Refrigerate
for four hours before serving with crackers. If dip is
too thick, add more ketchup.

# PARTY CHEESE BALL

8-oz. grated cheddar cheese
8-oz. softened cream cheese
1/2 med. onion, minced
2 T. dried chives, or 3 T.
   fresh, chopped fine
2 T. mayonnaise
1 c. nuts, well chopped

Mix together all ingredients (except the nuts) and form
a ball. Roll in the nuts until evenly coated. Chill until
serving time.

# CRAB SWISS BITES

1 pkg. refrigerator butterflake rolls
1 (7 1/2-oz.) can crabmeat, drained and flaked
1 (6-oz.) can water chestnuts, drained and diced
2 T. minced green onion, tops and bottoms
1 c. shredded Swiss cheese
1/2 c. mayonnaise
1/2 T. dill weed
1 tsp. lemon juice
Salt and pepper to taste

Separate each roll into three layers. Place on ungreased baking sheet. Mix all other ingredients together and then spoon onto top of each roll. Bake at 325°F for 15 to 20 minutes, checking to be sure they don't burn. May freeze before or after cooking. Makes 36 pieces.

# HAMBURGER DIP

1 1/2 lbs. ground beef
1 onion, chopped fine
1/2 lb. Velveeta cheese
1 small can mild green chilies

1 can refried beans
1 jar mild taco sauce
1 can cheddar cheese
  soup

Brown ground beef and onion together.  Drain off fat.
Put rest of ingredients with ground beef and onion in
crock-pot on low heat.  Serve with potato chips or nacho
cheese chips.

# PARTY HAM BALLS

2 1/2 lbs. ground smoked ham

3 lbs. ground beef

2 to 3 c. crushed graham crackers

4 eggs

1 c. milk

Combine ingredients; mix well. Shape into 1-inch balls.

## SAUCE:

2 cans tomato soup

2 1/4 c. brown sugar

3/4 c. vinegar

2 tsp. dry mustard

Combine ingredients for sauce; pour over meatballs. Bake at 300°F for 2 hrs. Serve warm or cold. Will freeze well. Makes 100 balls.

# FROSTED PECANS

1 egg white, beaten
  slightly
1 T. water
3 c. pecan halves
1/2 c. sugar

1/2 tsp. salt, or to taste
1 tsp. ground cinnamon
1/2 tsp. ground cloves
1/2 tsp. ground nutmeg

In a small bowl, beat together egg white and water until stiff. Stir in pecans, stirring until all surfaces are moistened. Mix together sugar, salt, and spices; sprinkle over pecans, mixing well. Spread pecans on a lightly greased or foil-lined cookie sheet; bake in preheated oven 30 minutes at 300° F. Stir twice to crisp and dry pecans evenly. Makes 3 cups.

# GUACAMOLE

3 ripe avocados
1 ripe tomato
Garlic powder to taste
Red salsa, add as much
  as you like

3 dashes Tabasco
1 tsp. lemon juice
Salt to taste
2 scallion onions,
  chopped

Peel avocados and remove pits. Mash fine. Remove seeds from tomato and chop into small pieces. Mix all ingredients together and chill. Serve with nacho chips and shredded cheddar or colby cheese.

# BLACK OLIVE CHEESE BALL

1 (8-oz.) pkg. cream
   cheese, softened
2 c. sharp cheddar
   cheese, shredded
1/2 c. ripe black olives,
   chopped

1/2 c. walnuts,
   finely chopped
1 T. minced parsley
1/2 tsp. lemon pepper
   seasoning
1/4 tsp. pepper sauce

Mix cream and cheddar cheese. Stir in rest of
ingredients. If a little more moisture is needed, use 1 T.
French dressing. Chill 1 hour; form into ball. Garnish
with nuts. Sprinkle with green parsley.

# MOM'S FRUIT DIP

1 (8-oz.) pkg. cream
  cheese
1/2 c. brown sugar

1/4 c. powdered
  sugar
1 tsp. vanilla

Beat all ingredients together with electric mixer. Better
if made day before serving. Especially good with apple
slices.

# ALASKA SALMON NUGGETS

1 lb. can salmon
1/2 c. mashed
   potatoes
1 T. finely minced
   celery
1 T. grated onion
1 egg, beaten
1 c. dry bread crumbs

1/4 tsp. salt
Dash pepper
1 1/2 tsp. Worcestershire
   sauce
1/4 lb. sharp Cheddar
   cheese
Bread crumbs

Drain and flake salmon. Combine all ingredients except cheese and bread crumbs, mix thoroughly. Shape into balls the size of walnuts. Cut cheese into 3/8-inch cubes. Insert a cube into center of each fish ball and reshape. Roll in bread crumbs. Fry in deep fat at 375°F for 3 to **4 minutes or until golden brown. Serves 6. <u>NOTE:</u>** Another kind of cheese may be substituted for the sharp Cheddar cheese.

# HOT CRAB MEAT DIP

1 (7-oz.) can crab meat
1 (8-oz.) pkg. cream
   cheese
1 T. mayonnaise
1-3 T. lemon juice

Garlic salt, to taste
1 T. chopped onion
Cheddar cheese,
   grated
Chives

Mix first six in order given and place in pie tin. Cover
with cheese and chives. Bake at 350°F for 30 min.
Serves 4. Serve with chips or crackers.

# TACO DIP

1 (16-oz.) can refried beans
1 (8-oz.) carton sour cream
1 pkg. taco seasoning
Cheddar cheese, shredded
Monterey Jack cheese,
   shredded

Tomatoes, chopped
Black olives,
   chopped
Taco salsa
   (mild or hot)
Tostitos or Doritos

Layer plate with refried beans. Mix sour cream and taco seasoning. Put on top of beans. Add as much cheese, tomatoes and olives as you like. Put salsa on top. Double recipe for a party.

# COCKABURS

12 oz. raw peanuts (1 1/2 c.)
1 c. sugar
1 c. water

Mix all together. Cook on medium heat on stove until liquid is dissolved. Spread on cookie sheet. Bake 350°F for 20 minutes. Take out of oven. May salt or leave unsalted. Bake 10 more min. If not salting, bake for total of 30 min. without removing from oven. Cool. Store in tight jar or container.

# GLAZED HOLIDAY PECANS

1 lb. pecan halves - Spread evenly in pan and put into 300° oven for 15 min.  Melt 1/4 c. butter; add 1/2 c. maple syrup and 1/4 tsp. salt.  Pour over toasted pecans and bake 15 min. or more at 300°.  Spread on brown paper sack.  Cool 10 min. and sprinkle with 1 T. sugar.

# TACO DIP

1 8-oz. pkg. cream cheese
1 6-oz. taco sauce (mild or hot)
1/2 tomato
1/2 green pepper
1/2 onion
Sharp cheddar cheese

Mix cream cheese and taco sauce with mixer or blender until smooth. Spread on plate. Cut up tomato, green pepper and onions; sprinkle on top of cheese mixture. Grate cheddar cheese and put on top. Place this plate on top of a larger plate and place Doritos around the edges.

When making this for a large crowd, use:
    4 (8-oz.) pkgs. cream cheese
    2 (12-oz.) bottles taco sauce (1 hot and 1 mild)

# SPINACH BALLS

3 c. herb seasoned
  stuffing mix
1 tsp. pepper
1 1/2 tsp. garlic salt
1 c. Parmesan cheese
1 large onion (diced)

3/4 c. melted butter
  or margarine
6 eggs
2 (10-oz.) pkg. frozen
  chopped spinach

Cook; drain spinach. Set aside to cool. Combine rest of ingredients in order given. Make into 3/4 to 1-inch balls. Place on lightly greased cookie sheet. Bake 325° for 20 minutes. Makes 40 balls.

# EASY CARAMEL POPCORN

| 1/2 c. unpopped corn | 3/4 c. packed brown sugar |
|---|---|
| 1 stick butter | 10 large marshmallows |

Pop corn usual way; get old maids out. Put popped corn in large bowl. Melt rest of ingredients in glass dish in microwave for 1 min. Stir; microwave for 2 more minutes. Stir until melted; pour over popped popcorn in large bowl. Mix until well coated. Put in a medium brown paper bag; microwave for 1 minute. Shake bag. Microwave for 1 more minutes. Pour onto wax paper.

# FANTASTIC PARTY MEATBALLS

1 pkg. any brand meatballs or your recipe
1 c. chili sauce
1 c. grape jelly

Heat meatballs according to package directions.
Meanwhile, in a small saucepan, combine chili sauce
and grape jelly. Heat until jelly is melted. Place
meatballs in a serving dish. Pour chili sauce mixture
over the meatballs; stir gently to coat. Serve warm.

# SOUPS, SALADS AND SIDE DISHES

# CAULIFLOWER OR BROCCOLI SOUP

4 T. margarine
2/3 c. chopped onion
3 T. flour
2 c. chopped, cooked
    cauliflower or broccoli

3 c. milk
1 can potato soup
4 slices of American
    cheese, cubed
Salt - pepper to taste

Melt margarine in saucepan. Add onion and cook until tender. Blend in flour; add cauliflower or broccoli, milk, soup, cheese, and seasonings. Cook until thick and cheese melts.

# TACO SOUP

1 lb. ground beef
1 onion, chopped
1 pkg. ranch-style
   dressing mix
1 pkg. taco
   seasoning mix
1 15-oz. can cream-style corn

1 c. water
2 14.5-oz. cans diced
   tomatoes with
   green chilies
2 15-oz. cans pinto beans
1 15-oz. can black beans

Brown beef with onions in a medium-size soup pot.
Drain excess grease. Add remaining ingredients;
simmer 20 minutes before serving.

# WILD RICE SOUP

6 T. butter or margarine
1 T. minced onion
1/2 c. flour
3 c. chicken broth
2 c. cooked wild rice

1/2 tsp. salt
1 c. Half & Half
2 T. dry sherry (opt.)
Snipped parsley or
   chives

Melt butter in saucepan; saute onion until tender.
Blend in flour; gradually stir in broth. Cook, stirring
constantly, until mixture comes to full boil; boil and stir
1 minute. Stir in rice and salt; simmer about 5 minutes.

Blend in Half & Half and sherry.  Heat to serving temperature.  Garnish with parsley.  Makes 5 cups.

**<u>Variation:</u>**  Add 1/3 c. minced ham, 1/3 c. finely shredded carrot and 3 T. chopped slivered almonds with rice and salt.

# CRANBERRY FLUFF

2 c. raw cranberries
3 c. miniature marshmallows
3/4 c. sugar
2 c. diced, unpeeled, red apples
1/2 c. seeded grapes
1 c. diced pineapple
1/2 c. pecan nuts
1 c. heavy cream or
    Cool Whip
1/4 c. mayonnaise

Put the cranberries through the grinder, using the coarse blade. Add marshmallows and sugar. Stir and let stand overnight. The next day, add the apples, grapes, pineapples, and nuts. Whip cream and add the mayonnaise to it. Fold gently into mixture. Serve in a lettuce cup. A good Christmas salad.

# LAYERED CRANBERRY SALAD

1 c. fresh cranberries
1/2 orange, unpeeled
1/3 c. sugar
1/2 tsp. cinnamon
1 pkg. (3-oz.) strawberry
   gelatin
1 1/2 c. hot water

1 pkg. 3-oz. lemon
   gelatin
1 c. hot water
1 T. lemon juice
1/3 c. orange juice
1 1/2 c. red or green
   grapes
1/2 c. sour cream

Put cranberries and orange thru medium blade of food grinder. Mix with sugar and cinnamon. Dissolve strawberry gelatin in 1 1/2 c. hot water. Swift chill in freezer 15 minutes. Stir in cranberry relish. Pour into 8-inch square pan or fancy 6-cup mold. Chill until firm. Dissolve lemon gelatin in 1 cup hot water; stir in lemon and orange juices. Chill until mix mounds on a spoon. Meanwhile, halve and seed grapes. Mix syrupy gelatin and sour cream. Fold in grapes. Pour over firm cranberry layer. Chill. Cut into squares or unmold and serve. No dressing needed. Serves 8 -10.

# BROCCOLI-DELIGHT SALAD

1 large bunch broccoli,
    cut in pieces
2 c. cauliflower
10 strips crisp bacon,
    crumbled
1 c. raisins

1/4 c. red onion, diced
1 c. sunflower seeds
1/2 c. lite mayonnaise
1/2 c. sour cream
3 to 4 T. sugar
1 T. vinegar

Wash and cut vegetables; add bacon, raisins, onion and seeds. Cream mayonnaise, sour cream, sugar and vinegar. Mix well and refrigerate until ready to eat.

# CRUNCHY PEA SALAD

1 pkg. (10-oz.) frozen peas, thawed
1 c. chopped cauliflower
1/2 c . sour cream (can use 1/2 and 1/2 sour cream, also)
1 c. prepared Hidden Valley Ranch Orig. Ranch salad dressing
1 c. chopped cashews

1 c. diced celery
Bacon Bits (2-oz.)
1/2 c. green onion, diced

Combine all ingredients. Chill. Add cashews just before serving or they get soft.

# FRUIT SALAD

2 cans pineapple tidbits
2 cans mandarin oranges
Orange juice as needed
1 pkg. orange tapioca pudding
1 pkg. vanilla tapioca pudding
1 c. whipping cream, whipped

Drain pineapple and mandarin oranges, saving juice
plus add enough orange juice to make 3 cups. Use this
to cook the two puddings. Cool. Fold in whipped
cream and fruit. Refrigerate.

# MOLDED GREEN SALAD

1 c. cottage cheese (large curd), rinsed
1 family size pkg. lime Jello
1 c. crushed pineapple, drained
1/2 c. sliced almonds
1 large pkg. Cool Whip

Mix above ingredients; pour into a mold or 9 by 13-inch pan. Refrigerate until set. Serves 15-20.

# GREEN PEA SALAD

1/2 c. sweet relish
No. 2 can of peas,
   drained
2 hard-cooked eggs

1/2 c. Velveeta, cubed
1/2 c. salad dressing
1/2 c. celery

Toss together and chill.  Serves six.

# SAUER SALAD

Bring to boil:  2 c. sugar, 1 c. white vinegar

    1 #2 1/2 can sauerkraut
    1 can drained bean sprouts
    2 c. chopped celery
    2 c. chopped onion
    1/2 c. diced bell pepper

Pour syrup over mixture, store in refrigerator at least 24 hours before using.  Will keep 2-3 weeks if sealed.

# CRANBERRY FRUIT SALAD

1 qt. cranberries, chopped, 2 large red apples, diced
small, and 1 1/2 c. sugar
Let stand overnight.

1 pkg. raspberry Jello, 1 3/4 c. boiling water
Cool, then add to apple-cranberry mixture.

When above is chilled, but not set, add:
    1/2 c. diced celery, 1/2 c. chopped nut meats

Pour into mold and let set.

# 24-HOUR VEGETABLE SALAD

1 head lettuce
1/2 c. diced celery
1/2 c. diced green pepper
1 (10-oz.) box frozen peas
1 red onion, thinly sliced
8 slices bacon, fried crisp and crumbled

2 T. sugar (opt.)
2 c. Miracle Whip
1 (4-oz.) pkg. grated
   cheddar cheese

Break lettuce in small pieces and crumbled in 9x13-inch
pan. Layer with celery, pepper, peas and onion. Frost
with Miracle Whip. Sprinkle top layer with grated
cheese and crumbled bacon. Cover; refrigerate 24 hrs.

# RASPBERRY SOUR CREAM SALAD

2 (8-oz.) pkgs. raspberry Jello
1 large can crushed pineapple
1 (8-oz.) carton sour cream
2 (10-oz.) pkgs. raspberries

Dissolve 1 pkg. Jello in 3 c. hot water. Drain; add 1/2 can pineapple and 1 pkg. raspberries. Pour into bottom of 9x13-inch baking dish. Let set till firm. Stir sour cream to make creamy and spread on top of set Jello.

Dissolve other pkg. of Jello and add remainder of pineapple and other pkg. of raspberries. Set in refrigerator till it is slightly congealed. Pour over sour cream and set up in refrigerator (Warm Jello will cause sour cream to rise.)

# EGGNOG RING

1 (3-oz.) pkg. lemon
  gelatin
1 c. boiling water
1/4 c. cold water
1/4 c. rum extract
3/4 c. canned eggnog

1 can mandarin
  oranges
1 (3-oz.) pkg. cherry
  gelatin
1 c. boiling water
1 1/2 c. pecans

Dissolve lemon gelatin in boiling water; add cold water
and rum extract. Measure 3/4 c. gelatin and pour into
another bowl. Add eggnog; set aside. Pour remaining
lemon gelatin with rum extract into 6-cup ring mold.

Chill until set but not firm, about 25 minutes. Drain mandarin oranges, measuring syrup. Add water to syrup to make 3/4 cup. Dissolve cherry gelatin in boiling water. Add measured liquid and remaining lemon gelatin. Pour into mold and chill until thick. Over eggnog-gelatin mixture, arrange oranges, pressing down lightly. Chill for 4 hours. Un-mold. Garnish with maraschino cherries. Fill center with 1 1/2 cups pecans.

# PINEAPPLE, MARSHMALLOW AND NUT SALAD

**Dressing:**

| | |
|---|---|
| 1/4 c. sugar | 1 egg |
| 1/2 tsp. salt | 2 T. vinegar |
| 1 1/2 T. flour | 3/4 c. pineapple juice |

Mix in order and cook over low heat, stirring constantly. Cool.

**Add:**

8-oz. chunk pineapple

1 c. miniature marshmallows

1/2 c. nuts

Stir and refrigerate until serving time.

# JIGGLERS

4 c. boiling water or boiling apple juice
   (Do not add cold water)
4 pkg. (4-serving size) Jell-O Brand Gelatin,
   any flavor

Stir boiling water or boiling juice into gelatin in large
bowl at least 3 min. until completely dissolved. Pour
into 13x9-inch pan or a mold. Refrigerate at least 3 hrs.
or until firm. Dip bottom of pan in warm water about
15 sec. Cut into decorative shapes with cookie cutters
all the way through gelatin. Lift from pan.

# CAULIFLOWER LAYER SALAD

1 head lettuce
1 head cauliflower
1 lb. bacon (fry crisp
   and break up or use
   bacon bits from jar)

1 med. chopped onion
1/2 c. sugar
1/3 c. parmesan cheese
Salt and pepper

Layer in large bowl; cover. Refrigerate overnight. Add 2 c. mayonnaise before serving; toss. Do not use Miracle Whip.

# TWENTY-FOUR HOUR SALAD

1 c. coconut
1 c. sour cream
1 c. pineapple chunk
1 c. mandarin oranges
1 c. miniature marshmallows

Put together and chill 24 hours.  Serves six.

# TRI-FRUIT SALAD

1 c. diced apples, unpeeled
1 c. diced bananas
1 T. lemon juice
1/2 c. pineapple bits, drained

1/2 c. raisins
1/2 c. coarsely chopped
   pecans
1/3 c. mayonnaise

Place apples, bananas and lemon juice in a bowl and toss. Add pineapple, raisins and pecans. Toss slightly. Add mayonnaise. Serves six.

# CRANBERRY SALAD

1/2 qt. raw cranberries
3 red apples, unpeeled
2 oranges, peeled
2 c. sugar
1/2 c. nuts

Grind cranberries and sprinkle sugar over them. Let stand two to three hours. Add chopped apples and oranges. Also, add nuts. Fold into one pkg. of strawberry or cherry gelatin which has been cooled.

# RED APPLE SALAD

4 firm tart apples
1 1/2 c. sugar
1/4 tsp. salt
1/2 c. red cinnamon
  candies

3 c. water
1/2 c. cottage cheese or
  3-4 oz. cream cheese
1/4 c. chopped green
  pepper

Pare and core apples. Add sugar, salt and candies to the water. Put over heat and stir until candies are dissolved. Cook apples slowly in this syrup in covered pan until just tender, turning occasionally to color evenly; drain and chill. Mix cheese with green pepper and stuff the apples. Serve on lettuce. Serves 4.

# FROSTED SALAD

1 pkg. lemon gelatin
1 c. boiling water
1 c. clear carbonated
  beverage
1 can (10-oz.) crushed
  pineapple

1/2 c. miniature
  marshmallows
1 large banana, sliced
Whipped Cream
  Topping

Dissolve gelatin in boiling water. Stir in carbonated beverage. Chill until partly set. Drain pineapple, saving juice for Whipped Cream Topping. Fold pineapple, marshmallows, and banana into gelatin. Chill until firm. Add topping. Chill overnight.

# WHIPPED CREAM TOPPING

1/4 c. sugar
1 T. flour
1/2 c. pineapple juice
1 egg, slightly beaten
1 T. butter

1/2 c. whipped cream
2 T. American cheese, shredded
1 1/2 T. grated Parmesan cheese

Combine sugar and flour in saucepan. Stir in pineapple juice and egg. Cook over low heat until thickened. Remove from heat; add butter. Let cool; chill. Fold into whipped cream. Frost gelatin mixture. Sprinkle on cheeses.

# NOODLE CASSEROLE

1 (10-oz.) pkg. frozen
   broccoli, thawed
1 (10-oz.) pkg. frozen
   cauliflower, thawed
1 pkg. frozen noodles
1 c. mushroom soup
1 1/2 c. shredded Swiss cheese

1 c. sour cream
1 red onion,
   chopped
1 tsp. salt
1/4 tsp. pepper

Cook noodles; drain and return to kettle. Add rest of ingredients. Put in casserole; mix gently. Bake 30 minutes at 350°.

# CHEESE POTATOES

3 T. melted butter           1 tsp. salt
4 med.-size boiled potatoes,    1/2 tsp. paprika
   peeled and sliced
1/4 c. finely crushed corn flakes
1/2 c. finely grated sharp process cheese

Pour 2 T. butter into shallow 11 x 7-inch baking pan. Place potatoes in baking pan. Brush tops with remaining butter. Combines corn flakes, cheese, salt, and paprika; sprinkle over the potatoes. Bake in hot oven (425°) about 15 minutes or until top is lightly browned.

# BROCCOLI AND WILD RICE BAKE

1 to 1/4 lb. fresh broccoli, cut in 1-inch pieces
6 3/4-oz. pkg. quick-cooking long-grain and wild
   rice mix
1 envelope sour cream sauce mix
1 single-serving envelope cream of mushroom
   soup mix
1/2 tsp. salt
2 c. milk
3/4 c. soft bread crumbs (1 slice bread)
1 T. butter or margarine, melted
1/4 tsp. paprika

Cook broccoli stem pieces, covered, in boiling salted water to cover, about 5 minutes. Add broccoli flowerets and cook 4 to 5 minutes more or till tender. Drain. Meanwhile, prepare rice mix according to pkg. directions. Combine dry sour cream sauce mix, dry mushroom soup mix, and salt; gradually stir in milk. Combine cooked rice and sour cream sauce mixture; fold in broccoli. Turn into 2-quart casserole. Combine bread crumbs, butter or margarine, and paprika; sprinkle atop. Bake, uncovered, in 350° oven for 20 to 25 minutes, or till heated through. Serves 8.

# RED CABBAGE WITH APPLES

2 - 2 1/2 lb. red cabbage
2/3 c. red wine vinegar
2 T. sugar
2 tsp. salt
2 T. bacon fat
2 med. cooking apples
  peeled, core and cut
  into 1/8-inch wedges

1/2 c. chopped onions
1 whole onion,
  peeled and pierced
  with 2 whole cloves
1 small bay leaf
5 c. boiling water
3 T. dry red wine
3 T. red current jelly

Shred cabbage into 1/8-inch strips. Drop cabbage in

large bowl. Sprinkle with vinegar, salt and sugar. Then toss to coat. Melt bacon fat in casserole over moderate heat. Cook apples and onions until lightly browned. Add cabbage, whole onion, and bay leaf. Stir thoroughly. Pour in water; bring to boil over high heat, stirring occasionally. Reduce heat to lowest possible point. Cover and simmer 1 1/2 to 2 hours. Check frequently. Add a tablespoon of water at a time if it seems dry. Before serving, remove onion and bay leaf; stir in wine and jelly. Serves 4.

# BEAN-POT BEANS

4 c. small white beans
1 lb. piece salt pork
1 large peeled onion
1 heaping tsp. mustard

1/2 c. molasses
1 T. salt
1 tsp. pepper

Let beans soak overnight. Cover with cold water; heat until a white scum appears. Drain water, place salt pork and sliced onion in bottom of pot. Pour in beans. Put on molasses, mustard and pepper and two T. of catsup, if desired. Fill with water; bake in slow oven. After two hours, add a tsp. of salt, dissolved in a cup of boiling water, to the beans. Every hour or so, add enough boiling water to replace what boiled away. Be sure cover is off last hour.

# SAVORY ONIONS

4 large onions - cut in slices, don't separate rings.

**<u>Boil together:</u>**

1/4 c. vinegar

1/4 c. sugar

1/4 c. water

1/2 c. butter

Pour over onions - bake covered at 350° for 1 hour.

# WILD RICE

| | |
|---|---|
| 1 lb. wild rice | 5 med. sized onions (diced) |
| 1 1/2 lb. cooked meat | 1 (4-oz.) can of mushrooms |
| (chicken or beef or both) | 8 slices of bread toasted |

Wash the rice and put in cold water; cool slowly until done. Then wash thoroughly again. Cook the meat until tender and save the broth to pour over the toast. Cook the onions until tender and drain. Now put altogether with mushrooms; mix well. Salt and pepper to suit your taste. Then place mixture in a greased baking dish and heat thoroughly in a moderate oven.

# GRANDMA'S DRESSING

| | |
|---|---|
| 1 loaf bread, cubed and laid out to dry (about 3 days) | 1 tsp. salt |
| | 1 3/4 to 2 c. milk |
| 1/2 c. butter, melted | 1 tsp. pepper |
| 1 med. or large onion | 1 egg |
| 1 T. poultry seasoning | 1 c. turkey broth |

Cook turkey and use the drippings to make broth. Much better than using store-bought chicken broth. Or if you cook a turkey earlier in the year, you can freeze the broth and use when desired or omit broth and use more milk. Stuff the turkey. In large roasting pan, mix all of the above ingredients.

# ONION RINGS

| | |
|---|---|
| 3/4 c. cornstarch | 1/4 tsp. pepper (opt.) |
| 1/4 c. flour | 1/2 c. water |
| 1 tsp. baking powder | 1 egg, slightly beaten |
| 1/2 tsp. salt | Onions |

Mix dry ingredients. Mix water and egg. Combine dry ingredients with water and egg. Dip sliced onions (sliced crosswise) into batter. Deep-fat fry at 375°F for two to three minutes. Make sure to turn onion rings while frying.

## SCALLOPED PINEAPPLE

1 c. butter or margarine
3 eggs
4 c. bread cubes

1 1/4 to 2 c. sugar
1 (20-oz.) can chunk
   pineapple

Mix together margarine, sugar and eggs.  Fold in the
pineapple and bread cubes.  Put mixture in 2 quart
casserole dish and bake at 350° for 30 - 45 minutes.

# CANDIED SWEET POTATOES

2 cans (1 lb. 7 oz.) sweet potatoes in extra heavy syrup.
Drain 1 can but use liquid of other can. Place in
casserole in one layer and add reserved juice. Pour 1
cup white sugar over potatoes and dot with oleo. Bake
for 2 hours in 350° oven.

(Can use fresh sweet potatoes but will need to peel and
boil them.) Use some of the liquid that you boiled them
in in place of one can of liquid. You may want to add
an extra 1/4 c. sugar.

# POTATOES AU GRATIN

2 (10 1/2-oz.) cans condensed
   Cheddar cheese soup
1 c. milk
8 c. potatoes (thinly sliced)
2 small onions (thinly sliced)

1 tsp. salt
2 T. butter <u>or</u>
   margarine
Paprika

Blend soup with milk and salt to make sauce. In a buttered 9 x 13 pan, arrange alternate layers of potatoes and onions and sauce. Dot top with butter and sprinkle generously with paprika. Cover; bake at 350° for 1 hour and 30 minutes. Uncover; bake 15 minutes longer or until potatoes are done. Serves 8 to 12.

# BREADS
## ROLLS AND
### MUFFINS

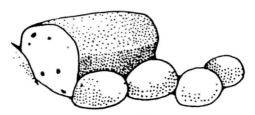

# POTATO PANCAKES

2 eggs
1/2 small onion
1 tsp. salt

2 T. flour
1/4 tsp. baking powder
3 c. cubed raw potatoes

Put first five ingredients and 1/2 c. potato cubes in blender. Cover and process at "grate" until potatoes have gone through the blades. Add remaining potatoes; cover and process at "chop" only until all potato cubes have passed through processing blades. Do not over-blend. Pour onto a hot well-greased griddle. Brown on both sides and serve hot.

# SOUR CREAM COFFEE CAKE

1/2 c. shortening
3/4 c. sugar
1 tsp. vanilla
3 eggs

2 c. flour
1 tsp. baking soda
1 tsp. baking powder
1 c. sour cream

Cream shortening, sugar and vanilla. Add eggs, beating after each one. Add sifted dry ingredients to mixture alternately with sour cream. Spread half of batter in greased tube pan.

**<u>Mix together:</u>**
6 T. butter or oleo, softened    1 c. brown sugar
2 tsp. cinnamon    1 c. nuts

Put half of this on batter.  Add remaining batter; then
rest of brown sugar mixture.  Bake at 350° for 45-50
minutes.  Glaze with powdered sugar frosting.

# MELT-IN-YOUR-MOUTH
# CHERRY-FILLED COFFEECAKE

3 c. flour
1 tsp. baking powder
1 tsp. baking soda
1 c. sugar
1 c. butter

2 eggs
1 c. sour cream
1 tsp. vanilla
1 can cherry pie
  filling

Combine first four ingredients. Add butter; cut in as
for pie dough until crumbs form. Add eggs, sour

cream, and vanilla. Mix until smooth. Spread 1/2 of batter into greased 9x13-inch pan. Spread cherries on top. Drop remaining batter on top.

## <u>CRUMB TOPPING:</u>

| | |
|---|---|
| 1/2 c. sugar | 2 T. melted butter |
| 1/2 c. flour | |

Combine topping ingredients and sprinkle on top of batter. Bake at 350° to 375°F for 40 minutes. Serve with Cool Whip.

# MARILYN'S CINNAMON ROLLS

2 pkgs. dry yeast
1/2 c. warm water
2 c. lukewarm milk (scalded
    then cooled)
1/3 c. sugar
1/3 c. vegetable oil
3 tsp. baking powder

2 tsp. salt
1 egg
5-6 c. flour
4 T. butter, softened
1/2 c. sugar
1 T. plus 1 tsp. cinnamon
Powdered Sugar Frosting

Dissolve yeast in warm water. Stir in milk, 1/3 c. sugar, oil, baking powder, salt, egg and 2-3 c. flour. Beat until smooth. Mix in enough remaining flour to make dough easy to handle. Put dough on well-floured board; knead

8-10 min. until smooth and elastic. Place in greased bowl; turn greased side up. Cover; let rise in warm place until double, about 1 1/2 hr. Grease 2 pans, 13x9x2 in. Punch down dough; divide into halves. Roll one half into 12x10 in. rectangle. Spread on half the butter. Mix 1/2 c. sugar with the cinnamon; sprinkle 1/2 sugar-cinnamon mixture over rectangle. Roll up, beginning at wide side. Pinch edges of dough into roll; seal. Stretch roll to make even. Cut roll into 12 slices; place in pan. Do same with other half; let rise 30 min. Bake at 350° for 30-35 min. Frost with powdered sugar frosting while warm. For frosting, mix 2 c. powdered sugar, 2 T. milk & 2 tsp. vanilla until smooth and spreads easily. Recipe makes 24 rolls.

# CHRISTMAS CROCK

| | |
|---|---|
| 1 lb. butter | 1/2 tsp. baking soda |
| 3 c. sugar | 1/2 tsp. salt |
| 5 eggs, separated | 1 tsp. vanilla |
| 1 c. buttermilk | 3 (10-oz.) bottles |
| 5 c. flour | maraschino cherries |
| 1 lb. whole Brazil nuts or walnuts | |

Cream butter and sugar. Add beaten egg yolks. Add buttermilk and flour/soda/salt mixture alternately. Add vanilla. Fold in stiffly beaten egg whites. Add cherries, drained of juice (can use red and green cherries). Add 1 lb. of Brazil nuts or walnuts. Bake in 4 large, or 5 small, loaf pans for 1 hr. at 350°F. To prepare pans, grease pan; put layer of brown paper in bottom, grease again. Freezes well.

# YULE KAKE (YEAST SWEET ROLL RECIPE)

Scald 2 c. milk; cool to lukewarm.

**Add:**
   1 c. warm water
   2 yeast pkg.
   2 T. sugar

Dissolve and add to milk.

**Add:**
   2/3 c. (scant) melted shortening
   2 beaten eggs

93

1/2 c. sugar
4 tsp. salt

And then add:

1 lb. chopped dates
1 c. coarse chopped nuts
Red and green candied cherries.

Last add enough flour to work easily. Knead
8-10 minutes.

Let rise in warm place for about one hour or until
double in size. Punch down and form in three balls.
Let rise until double. Bake at 325° for approximately
40-50 minutes. Frost with powdered sugar frosting.

# ORANGE ROLLS

### For the dough:

1 qt. milk, scalded and cooled
1 c. mashed potatoes, pushed through a sieve to get all the lumps out
1 c. sugar
1/2 c. melted Crisco, not hot
2 cakes yeast, dissolved in 1/2 c. cold water
2 tsp. salt
1 tsp. soda
2 tsp. baking powder
2 qt. wheat flour, plus enough more to make the dough stiff, but not sticky in the mixer bowl.

Combine it all with the cooled milk; let rise somewhere warm. After rising, put it in refrigerator covered well.

### For the orange filling:

Grind rind of two oranges. Mix with 1 c. sugar; let stand 12 hours. Roll like a jelly roll; cut in 1-in. slices. Bake at 425° for 12-15 min. Just before taking from oven, pour orange glaze over the rolls.

### For the glaze:

1/2 c. white Karo syrup

1 c. sugar

1/2 c. hot water

Boil for a few minutes; then add the rind of one orange, grated, and let stand. (Best if made the day before.)

# RAW APPLE BREAD

1/2 c. oil
2 eggs
1 c. sugar
1 1/2 c. flour
1/2 tsp. baking soda
1 1/2 c. diced peeled apples

1/4 tsp. salt
1/2 c. chopped nuts
1 tsp. vanilla
1/2 tsp. cinnamon
1/2 tsp. nutmeg

Mix first three ingredients together. Add remaining ingredients and mix. Turn into greased and floured 8x4-inch loaf pan. Bake at 300°F for 1 1/2 hrs. Cool 10 min. Remove from pan. Wrap in foil while still warm.

# DEE'S DINNER ROLLS

3 pkg. yeast

3 c. lukewarm water

3/4 c. oleo

3/4 c. sugar

3 eggs, beaten

2 tsp. salt

9 1/4 c. sifted flour

Dissolve yeast in lukewarm water. Combine oleo and sugar. Stir in yeast mixture; add salt and flour alternately with beaten eggs. Let rise at room temperature until doubled. Shape and place in lightly greased pans; let rise again until doubled. Bake at 425° about 10 min. Makes 6 dozen rolls.

# APPLESAUCE-CARROT MUFFINS

1/2 c. raisins
1 c. flour
3/4 c. whole wheat flour
1 tsp. baking soda
1/2 tsp. salt
1 tsp. cinnamon
1/2 tsp. nutmeg

1 large egg
1/2 c. sugar
1/4 c. oil
1 tsp. vanilla
1/4 tsp. lemon extract
1 c. applesauce
3/4 c. grated carrots

Combine raisins with 1/2 c. warm water in small bowl;
let soak.  Mix flours, soda, salt, and spices in large bowl.

Beat egg and sugar in second bowl until fluffy; beat in oil, vanilla, and lemon. Stir in applesauce. Stir applesauce mixture into flour until just blended. Quickly fold in carrots and raisins with water; spoon into greased or sprayed muffin tins. Bake at 400°F for 15 to 18 minutes. Makes 12 large muffins.

# KOLACHES

| | |
|---|---|
| 1 c. butter (not margarine) | 1/2 c. sugar |
| 2 c. milk | 1 tsp. salt |
| 4 eggs | 6 to 6 1/2 c. flour |
| 2 pkgs. yeast | |

Heat together the butter and milk until a little more than lukewarm. Add eggs, yeast, sugar, salt and 3 c. flour; let rise. Add rest of flour; let rise again. Roll to 1/4 in. thickness. Let stand 10 min.; cut with cookie cutter. Let rise until double. Brush with melted butter. Indent center; fill with apricot or prune filling. Bake at 425°F for 10-15 min. Brush w/melted butter; sprinkle with coconut, nuts or graham cracker crumbs.

# MEATS AND MAIN DISHES

# SLOPPY JOES

4 lb. ground beef
1 med. onion, chopped
4 c. ketchup
1 oz. chili powder
12-oz. tomato juice
1 sleeve (1/4 lb.) saltine crackers, crumbled

Brown beef and onion in large pot; drain excess grease.
Stir in remaining ingredients. Simmer until thick. If
sauce is too thick, add 1/2-cup tomato juice or water.
Serves 20.

# BREAKFAST CASSEROLE

6 slices of bread, crumbled
8 eggs
1 c. milk
1/2 tsp. dry mustard
1/2 tsp. Worchestershire sauce
1 lb. cooked sausage
8 oz. shredded cheddar cheese
Crumbled bacon for topping

Spray a 13x9-inch cake pan or Pyrex baking dish with non-stick spray; sprinkle bread crumbs over entire bottom of dish.  Cover with cooked crumbed sausage.

Sprinkle with cheese; cover with eggs-milk-mustard-
Worcestershire-that have been all mixed together.
Cover and place in fridge.  Let sit in fridge overnight.
Bake at 350° for 45 minutes to one hour ( uncovered).
Sprinkle with cooked bacon as garnish.  Serve with
fresh fruit, cinnamon rolls or hotcakes!

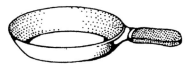

# ROAST GOOSE WITH APPLE, RAISIN AND NUT STUFFING

8-10 lb. goose
1 c. raisins
3 T. butter
1 c. finely chopped
   onions
4 c. soft bread crumbs
1 tsp. salt
Pepper to taste

3 med. cooking apples
   peeled, cored and
   coarsely chopped
1/2 c. chopped blanched
   hazelnuts or almonds
1/4 c. chopped parsley
1 tsp. dried marjoram

Mix butter, bread crumbs, onions, raisins, apples and nuts. Add parsley, marjoram, salt and pepper. If more moisture is needed, add hot water or chicken broth. Stuff goose with mixture. Place stuffed goose in roaster. Pour 2 cups boiling water over goose. Cover; bake at 325° for 25-30 minutes per lb. Roast uncovered last 15 minutes.

# STUFFED GREEN PEPPERS

6 large green peppers
1 1/2 lb. ground beef
1/4 c. vegetable oil
1/2 tsp. salt
1/4 tsp. pepper
3/4 tsp. ground oregano
1 1/2 c. cooked rice

1 (16-oz.) can diced,
   stewed tomatoes
1 corn, drained
1/4 c. minced onion
1 (15-oz.) can tomato
   sauce
1/4 c. water

Grease a 2 1/2-quart baking dish. Cut top from peppers; remove seeds. Rinse. Drop peppers in boiling

water; simmer 5 minutes.  Remove.  Set aside to drain.
Brown ground beef in oil; stir in salt, pepper, oregano,
cooked rice, stewed tomatoes and corn.  Fill pepper
shells, heaping slightly (put any extra stuffing along
side).  Combine tomato sauce, onion and water.  Pour
over peppers.  Top with cheese and sprinkle with
oregano.  Bake for 30 to 40 minutes (until peppers are
tender) in a 350°F oven.  Serves 4 to 6.

# BARBECUED POT ROAST

2 T. salad oil
1 (5-lb.) beef chuck roast
2 medium onions
1 garlic clove, minced
1 (8-oz.) can tomato sauce
1 (6-oz.) can tomato paste
2/3 c. packed light
  brown sugar

1/2 c. cider vinegar
1 T. salt
2 T. Worcestershire sauce
1/4 tsp. pepper
1/4 tsp. dry mustard
2 bay leaves
Parsley for garnish

In an 8-quart Dutch oven, over medium-high heat, in hot salad oil, cook pot roast until well browned on both sides. Remove meat to platter. In same Dutch oven, over medium heat, in drippings, cook onions and garlic until lightly browned, about 5 minutes, stirring occasionally. Spoon off drippings from Dutch oven. Stir in tomato sauce and remaining ingredients, except parsley. Return meat to Dutch oven. Over high heat, heat to boiling. Reduce heat to low; cover and simmer 3 1/4 hours, or until meat is fork-tender, turning meat once. Makes 10 to 12 servings.

# CHINESE SALAD WITH CHICKEN

Broil 2 boned (whole) chicken breasts which have been brushed with soy sauce. Chunk chicken before placing in salad.

Toss:
24 snow peas (pods)
1/4 head red cabbage
1 whole head lettuce, broken up
1 green pepper, chopped
2 cans mandarin oranges

**Brown in 2 T. oil:  1/2 c. slivered almonds (flat ones)**
**1 pkg. Ramen noodles**

**Serve with poppyseed dressing.**

# HAM ROLLS

2 1/2 lbs. ground ham
2 lbs. lean pork
3 c. crushed graham crackers

2 c. milk
3 eggs, slightly
   beaten

Mix above and form from 1/2 measuring cup into rolls.
**<u>SAUCE:</u>**
2 cans tomato soup
3/4 c. vinegar

2 1/4 c. brown sugar
2 tsp. dry mustard

Mix thoroughly and pour over the rolls. Bake at 350°
for 45 minutes.

# HOT CHICKEN SALAD

2 1/2 c. diced leftover cooked chicken (or turkey)
1 1/2 c. diced celery
1 c. mayonnaise
1/2 c. sliced almonds
2 T. lemon juice
1 T. grated onion
Potato chips and grated cheese

Combine first six ingredients; pour into casserole.
Cover with crushed potato chips, and strew with grated
cheese. Bake 30 min. at 350°.

# BEEF TIPS ON RICE

2 lbs. sirloin steak, cut
   in 1-inch cubes
1 (10-oz.) can beef
   consomme
1 c. water
2 T. soy sauce

Garlic salt, to taste
Onion salt, to taste
2 T. cornstarch
1/4 c. water
1 can mushrooms (opt)

117

Brown steak.  Add consomme, water, soy sauce and garlic and onion salts.  Heat to boiling and simmer 1 hour.  Blend cornstarch and water.  Add to above, stirring constantly, as it comes to a boil  Add mushrooms,  Serve on cooked rice.

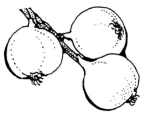

# SALMON LOAF

1 can salmon
2 eggs
1 c. rich milk
Pinch of salt

Pinch of pepper
1/2 c. bread crumbs
Onion, diced
1 T. flour
Dill weed (opt.)

Mix in order given. Put in greased loaf pan. Bake 30 to 40 minutes. Makes 6 to 8 servings.

# ENCHILADA CASSEROLE

2 lbs. ground beef
1 large onion
1 (6-oz.) can tomato sauce
1 large can enchilada sauce
1 c. water

1 lb. grated Cheddar cheese
2 sm. cans chopped black
  olives
1 can baked beans
12 corn tortillas

Brown meat and onion. Add tomato sauce, enchilada sauce and water; bring to a boil. Put a layer of sauce in large casserole and cover with 3 tortillas. Cover with 1/4 of cheese and olives. Repeat for four layers. Pour baked beans over top. Bake 1 hr. at 325°F. Serves 8.

# PIES, CAKES AND OTHER DESSERTS

# RITA'S SILK CHOCOLATE PIE FILLING

1/4 c. sugar
3 T. cornstarch
1 1/2 c. milk
1 (6-oz.) pkg. semi-sweet chocolate chips
1 tsp. vanilla
3/4 c. heavy cream
1 T. confectioners' sugar

In a medium saucepan, combine sugar and cornstarch, blend well. Gradually add milk; cook over medium heat, stirring constantly until mixture boils. Add chocolate chips and vanilla, stirring until melted and smooth. Pour into a large mixing bowl, cover with plastic wrap and cool to room temperature. In large bowl of mixer, combine heavy cream and confectioners' sugar. Beat until soft peaks form. Beat cooled chocolate mixture at medium speed, about 1 minute, until light and fluffy; fold into whipped cream. Spoon into crust (or glasses). Chill 2 to 3 hours. Serves 10.

# EXCELLENT PIE CRUST

6 c. flour
2 c. shortening
2 tsp. salt
2 well-beaten eggs

2 tsp. vinegar
Enough ice water to
make dough easy
to handle

Combine sifted flour and salt. Cut in 1 1/2 c. shortening until mixture resembles coarse meal. Then cut in additional 1/2 c. shortening until mixture particles are size of large peas. Then add eggs, vinegar and water. Bake at 400°. Makes four double crusts or eight single crusts.

# CRUSTLESS APPLE PIE

| | |
|---|---|
| 1 egg | Pinch of salt |
| 1/2 c. brown sugar | 1 tsp. baking powder |
| 1/2 c. white sugar | 4 medium-size apples |
| 1 tsp. vanilla |   pared and sliced |
| 1/2 c. flour | 1/2 c. nuts |

Beat egg in a medium-size bowl. Add brown sugar, sugar and vanilla. Sift flour with salt and baking powder; sift into egg mixture. Stir in apples and nuts. Bake in greased 9-inch pie pan for 30 minutes. Serve with whipped cream.

# SOUR CREAM RAISIN PIE

2 c. sour cream
1 c. sugar
2 c. raisins
1 tsp. cinnamon
3 egg yolks, beaten
Pinch salt

Mix ingredients.  Bring to a boil.  Cook 5 min.  Pour into baked pie shell.  Serve with whipped cream topping.

# SOUTHERN PECAN PIE

9-inch pie shell
1 c. pecan halves
3 eggs
1 T. melted butter

1 c. light corn syrup
1/2 tsp. vanilla
1 c. sugar
1 T. flour

Arrange the pecan halves in the bottom of the pie shell.
Beat the eggs; add the butter, corn syrup and vanilla.
Stir until well blended. Combine the sugar and flour
and blend this with the egg mixture. Pour over nuts in
the pie shell. Let stand until the nuts rise to the surface.
Bake in moderate oven, 350° for 45 min. The nuts will
glaze during baking. Serves six.

## PEANUT BUTTER PIE

1 qt. ice cream                    1/4 c. Karo (white) syrup
1/2 c. peanut butter

Soften ice cream, beat peanut butter and syrup into it. Pour in graham cracker crust; freeze. Top with hot fudge sauce.

## HOT FUDGE SAUCE

1 c. water                         1/4 c. cocoa
2 T. cornstarch                    1 c. sugar

Combine ingredients; cook until thick. Remove from heat, and add 1 T. butter and 1 tsp. vanilla. **NOTE:** Works well to cook in microwave. Never gets sugary.

# NOBBY APPLE CAKE

3 T. butter

1 c. sugar

1 egg, beaten

1/2 tsp. cinnamon

1/2 tsp. nutmeg

1/2 tsp. salt

1 tsp. baking soda

1 c. sifted flour

3 c. diced apples

1/4 c. chopped nuts

1 tsp. vanilla

Cream butter and sugar. Add egg. Mix well. Sift dry ingredients together. Add to creamed mixture. Stir in apple, nuts, and vanilla. Pour into greased 8x8x2 pan. Bake at 350° for 40 to 45 minutes. Serve hot or cold with whipped cream or ice cream.

# TEXAS CAKE

Sift together 2 c. flour and 2 c. sugar.
Bring to boil: 4 T. cocoa
               1 stick oleo
               1/2 c. shortening
               1 c. water
Pour over flour and sugar mixture.
Mix in: 1/2 c. sour milk    2 eggs
        1 tsp. soda          1 tsp. cinnamon
        1 tsp. vanilla      Pinch of salt
Pour into 2 (9x13) pans. Bake at 400° for 20 minutes.
Frost when cool with the following frosting:

131

## FROSTING

1 stick oleo
6 T. milk
4 T. cocoa

Bring to quick boil: Pour above 1 lb. powdered sugar.
Add 1 tsp. vanilla. Pour frosting on cake when it comes
from the oven. Add nuts.

# GRASSHOPPER DESSERT

Melt and cool:

> 30 marshmallows (reg. size)
>
> 3/4 c. milk

Fold 1 c. cream, whipped, into marshmallows and milk.

Add:  1 1/4 oz. creme de menth (2 T. = 1 oz.)

> 3/4 oz. creme de cocoa

Line 13 x 9 cake pan with crushed chocolate wafers, reserving some for top.  Pour filling on top of crushed wafers in pan.  Sprinkle remainder of crushed wafers on top.  Chill.

# MAGIC LEMON DESSERT

3/4 c. white sugar
2 T. butter
3 egg yolks
4 T. flour
Juice and rind of 1 large lemon
1 c. milk
3 egg whites beaten stiff and folded in last

Mix together in the order given. Pour into slightly buttered pan; bake at 370° for 25 minutes. Put smaller pan into a larger one which has a small amount of hot water in it to bake. The lemon layer goes to the bottom and the crust to the top.

# KANSAS DIRT CAKE

1 lg. pkg. Oreo cookies, crushed
1 (8-oz.) cream cheese, softened
1/2 c. margarine
1 c. powdered sugar
1 lg. Cool Whip
3 c. milk
2 (3 1/2 oz.) instant vanilla or
   chocolate pudding
1 tsp. vanilla

Put half of cookie crumbs in bottom of 13x9 pan. Beat cream cheese and margarine with electric mixer until smooth. Mix in powdered sugar. Fold in Cool Whip.

In separate bowl, mix instant pudding, milk and vanilla. Fold cream cheese mixture and pudding mixture together. Pour over cookie crumbs and sprinkle remaining crumbs on top. Chill over-night or freeze. Can be served frozen or chilled.

# POOR MAN'S FRUIT CAKE

**Bring to boil and simmer 5 minutes; then cool to lukewarm:**

     2 c. white raisins
     2 c. sugar
     2 T. shortening
     2 c. water

**Sift together:**

| | |
|---|---|
| 3 c. flour | 1 tsp. baking powder |
| 1/2 tsp. cloves | 1/2 tsp. nutmeg |
| 1 tsp. cinnamon | 3/4 tsp. salt |
| 1 tsp. allspice | |

Add fruit mixture to flour mix. Blend well, add 1 tsp. vanilla and 2 c. chopped nuts. Pour into greased paper lined pans and bake at 300° for 1 1 /2 hours. Place a pan of water in lowest grate of oven to keep moist.

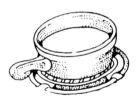

# MILE-HI STRAWBERRY DESSERT

## CRUST:

| | |
|---|---|
| 1/2 c. butter | 1 c. flour |
| 1/4 c. brown sugar | 1/2 c. nuts |

Mix; crumble into 13x9 pan. Bake 15 min. at 350°. Stir when half done; cool. Crumble again; save 1/3 for topping. Spread rest evenly in pan.

## FILLING:

| | |
|---|---|
| 10-oz. pkg. frozen straw-<br>   berries, partly thawed | 1/2 c. sugar |
| 2 egg whites, beaten | 1 T. lemon juice |

Beat 15-20 minutes in large bowl. Well get thick and fluffy. Whip 1/2 pt. whipping cream and fold into mixture. Pour over crust; top with remaining crust mixture. Freeze. Serve partly thawed. Serves 15-20.

# RASPBERRY LAYERED DESSERT

1 1/2 c. crushed pretzels (fig. 8)
3/4 melted butter
2 T. sugar
1 (9-oz.) carton Cool Whip
1 (8-oz.) pkg. cream cheese, softened
1 c. sugar

Mix first three ingredients. Pat into 9x13-inch pan.
Bake 10 minutes in a 350° oven. Blend cream cheese
and sugar. Fold in Cool Whip. Place on top crust.
Cool in refrigerator.

Mix:  2-3 oz. pkg. raspberry gelatin
      2 c. boiling hot water
      2 (10-oz.) pkg. frozen raspberry
        (partially thawed)

**Put on top of cream cheese and let set over night.**

# CREAMY STRAWBERRY CRUNCH

1/2 c. fine corn
  flake crumbs
2 T. sugar
2 T. finely chopped
  almonds
3 T. soft butter
1 T. unflavored
  gelatin

1/3 water
1 2/3 c. (1 tall can)
  evaporated milk
1/3 c. sugar
1/4 tsp. salt
1/2 tsp. almond
  flavoring
1 c. sweetened,
  sliced strawberries

Combine corn flake crumbs, sugar, almonds and butter. Mix well. Press evenly and firmly onto bottom of 1-quart ice cube tray, reserving 2 T. crumb mixture for topping, if desired. Chill.

Soften gelatin in water. Scald evaporated milk. Remove from heat and add softened gelatin, sugar, salt and almond flavoring. Stir until gelatin dissolves.

Chill mixture until it thickens slightly, then fold in drained strawberries. Pour into crumb-lined tray; top with reserved crumbs and chill until firm. Cut in bars or pie-shaped wedges. Makes 6 to 8 servings.

# CRANBERRY VELVET

1/2 lb. (2 cups)
  cranberries
1/2 c. water
2 tsp. unflavored gelatin
1/4 c. orange juice
2/3 c. sugar

1/2 - 1 tsp. grated
  orange peel
1/4 tsp. salt
2 egg whites
1/2 c. heavy cream
  whipped

Cook cranberries in water till skins pop; put through a food mill or sieve.  Soften gelatin in orange juice; add with 1/3 c. sugar to hot cranberry mixture, stirring till gelatin dissolves. Add peel and salt. Chill till partially set. Beat whites till soft peaks form; gradually add 1/3 c. sugar, beating to stiff peaks; fold into cranberry mixture. Fold in whipped cream. Pile into 6 to 8 sherbets. Chill till firm. Top with additional whipped cream.

# CRANBERRY APPLE CRUNCH

1 c. sugar
1 c. water
2 c. cranberries
2 c. chopped tart apples
1 recipe Topper

Mix sugar and water; boil 5 min. Add cranberries; cook 5 min. till skins pop. Remove from heat. Add apples; pour into buttered 10x6x1 1/2-inch baking dish. Sprinkle with Topper: Mix 1 c. quick-cooking rolled oats, 1/2 c. brown sugar, 1/3 enriched flour, and 1/2 tsp. salt. Cut in 1/4 c. butter or margarine till crumbly. Add 1/2 c. broken walnuts. Bake at 350° about 35 min. Cut in 6 to 8 squares. Serve warm with whipped cream.

# COOKIES AND BARS

# ANGEL COOKIES

| | |
|---|---|
| 1/2 c. brown sugar | 1 tsp. vanilla |
| 1/2 c. white sugar | 2 c. flour |
| 1 c. oleo | 1 tsp. soda |
| 1/2 tsp. salt | 1 tsp. cream of tarter |
| 1 egg | Coconut or nuts (opt.) |

Cream together first four ingredients; then add egg and vanilla. Sift flour, soda and cream of tarter together. Stir in finely cut coconut or nuts.

Roll into balls size of large marble. Moisten half of ball in cold water; dip in sugar. Bake 12 minutes at 350°.

# PEALING BELLS

2 c. flour
1 1/2 tsp. baking powder
6 T. butter or margarine
1/3 c. shortening
3/4 c. sugar
1 tsp. grated orange peel

1 T. milk
1 egg
1 tsp. vanilla
25 maraschino
   cherries, halved
   & well drained

Combine flour and baking powder. In a large mixer
bowl, beat butter and shortening until softened. Add
sugar; beat until fluffy. Add orange peel, milk, egg,

and vanilla; beat well. Add flour mixture; beat until well mixed. Shape into a roll; wrap and chill for several hours or overnight. Cut into 1/4-inch slices. Place on ungreased cookie sheet. Place a cherry on the bottom half of each slice for bell clapper. Fold in sides, slightly covering cherry to resemble bell. Bake at 350° 12 to 14 minutes.

# RIBBON COOKIES

| | |
|---|---|
| 1 c. oleo | 2 1/2 c. flour |
| 1 1/4 c. sugar | 1 1/2 tsp. baking powder |
| 1 egg | 1/4 c. chopped cherries |
| 1 tsp. vanilla | 1/4 c. nuts (opt.) |
| Pinch of salt | 1/4 c. candied pineapple |

Cream shortening and sugar; add egg and vanilla and beat well. Add dry ingredients; mix. Divide into three parts. Add cherries to one part and color red. Add nuts to one part. Add pineapple and color green to third part.

153

## Loaf pan:

Line with foil to cover; put layers one at a time in pan - red, white, and green.  Cover and chill overnight.  Cut into thin slices.  Bake at 375° for 10-12 minutes on greased cookie sheet.  Do not brown.

# JUMBO CHRISTMAS MUD SQUARES

3/4 c. graham cracker crumbs
3/4 c. finely chopped pecans
1/4 c. packed brown sugar
1/4 c. butter, melted

1 (12-oz.) jar caramel-flavored topping
3 T. flour

Combine first four ingredients, stirring well. Press crumb mixture into bottom of a greased 9-inch square pan. Bake at 350°F for 6 to 8 min. Cool slightly. Combine caramel and flour, stirring well. Spread on crust to within 1/4-inch from edge of pan. Set aside.

## Next layer:

1 c. butter

4 (1-oz.) squares un-
sweetened chocolate

1 1/2 c. sugar

1 c. flour

4 eggs, beaten

1 tsp. vanilla extract

Combine butter and chocolate in a heavy pan; cook over low heat until melted. Stir in sugar and next three ingredients. Pour mixture over caramel topping in pan. Bake at 350°F for 50 minutes. Cool slightly and spread with chocolate frosting.

# SWISS CINNAMON STARS

| | |
|---|---|
| 3/4 c. butter | 2 tsp. lemon juice |
| 1/2 c. granulated sugar | 1 c. coconut |
| 1 egg | 2 egg whites |
| 2 1/4 c. flour | 2 c. sifted confectioners' sugar |
| 2 tsp. cinnamon | Food coloring, if desired |
| 1/4 tsp. mace | |

Cream butter. Gradually add granulated sugar; cream until light and fluffy. Add egg and beat well. Combine flour with cinnamon and mace. Add to butter mixture, a small amount at a time, mixing thoroughly after each addition.  Blend in lemon juice and coconut.  Divide dough in two parts and wrap each in wax paper.  Chill 30  minutes or longer.

To make icing, beat egg whites until stiff.  Add confectioners' sugar, 2 T. at a time, beating thoroughly after each addition.  Continue beating until mixture is stiff and glossy.  Blend in few drops of food coloring, if desired.  Roll chilled dough to thickness of about 1/4-inch.  Cut out with star-shaped cutter.  Spread each cookie with about 1 tsp. icing.  Bake on ungreased baking sheet at 300° 15 to 18 min. or until cookie base is light brown.  Makes about 5 dozen.

# CUT-OUT SUGAR COOKIES

2/3 c. shortening
3/4 c. sugar
1 egg
1/2 tsp. vanilla
2 tsp. grated
   orange peel

2 c. sifted enriched
   flour
1 1/2 tsp. baking
   powder
1/4 tsp. salt
4 tsp. milk

Thoroughly cream shortening and sugar. Add egg; beat until mixture is light and fluffy. Add vanilla and grated orange peel; mix thoroughly. Sift dry ingredients; stir into creamed mixture together with milk. Divide dough in half. Chill 1 hour so it's easy to handle. Roll out one half, keeping the other chilled till you're ready to roll it. Roll dough 1/8-inch thick. Cut; put on greased cookie sheet; sprinkle lightly with sugar; bake in oven at (375°) for 12 minutes. Makes 2 dozen.

# PECAN TASSIES

## PASTRY:

1 (3-oz.) pkg. cream cheese          1 stick butter
1 c. flour

Cream soft cream cheese and butter; add flour. Chill
for 1 hour. Shape into 2 dozen balls; place in 1 3/4-inch
muffin pan. Press dough evenly against bottom and
sides of each.

## FILLING:

| | |
|---|---|
| 1 egg | 1/2 tsp. vanilla |
| 1 c. brown sugar | Dash of salt |
| 1 T. softened butter | |
| 2/3 c. coarsely broken pecans | |

Beat together egg, brown sugar, butter, vanilla and salt until smooth. Divide half of the pecans among pastry-lined pans; add egg mixture and top with remaining pecans. Bake at 325°F for 25 minutes. Let filling cool a while before removing from pan. Makes 2 dozen.

# DROP SUGAR COOKIES

| | |
|---|---|
| 1 c. margarine | 3 1/2 c. flour |
| 1 1/2 c. sugar | 1 tsp. nutmeg |
| 2 eggs | 1 tsp. vanilla |

2 T. milk with 1 tsp. baking soda dissolved in it

Beat margarine, sugar, and eggs until creamy; add milk with baking soda. Mix well. Add the flour, nutmeg, and vanilla; mix well. Chill for a day. Take out; roll into balls the size of a walnut. Bake 10-12 min. in 350°F oven. Flatten out with a glass dipped in sugar. Dough can be kept in refrigerator several days before baking.

# ONE-CUP-OF-EVERYTHING COOKIES

1 c. granulated sugar
1 c. brown sugar
1 c. butter
1 c. oil
1 c. oatmeal
1 c. coconut
1 c. rice krispies

1 egg
1 tsp. baking soda
1 tsp. cream of tarter
1/2 tsp. salt
1 tsp. cinnamon
3 1/2 c. flour
1/2 c. chopped nuts

Mix all ingredients together in large bowl, then roll into balls. Roll in granulated sugar. Bake 10 min. at 350°F.

# SUNFLOWER SEED COOKIES

| | |
|---|---|
| 3 eggs, beaten | 2 1/2 c. flour |
| 1 tsp. vanilla | 1 tsp. cinnamon |
| 1 c. white raisins | 2 tsp. baking soda |
| 1 c. Crisco | 1/2 tsp. salt |
| 1 c. brown sugar | 2 c. quick oatmeal |
| 1 c. granulated sugar | 1/2 c. sunflower kernels |

Combine eggs, vanilla, and raisins; let stand for 1 hour. Cream shortening; add sugars and egg mixture. Add flour, baking soda, cinnamon, salt, and oatmeal. Stir in sunflower kernels. Chill 1 hour. Roll in balls; place on cookie sheet. Bake at 350°F for 15 min. Makes 5 dozen.

# PEANUT BUTTER BLOSSOMS

1 c. sugar
1 c. brown sugar
1 c. shortening
1 c. peanut butter
2 eggs

4 T. milk
1 tsp. vanilla
2 tsp. soda
3 3/4 to 4 c. flour
1/2 tsp. salt

Mix well. Make dough into balls size of walnuts. Roll balls in sugar and bake at 375° approximately 8-10 minutes till barely done. Remove from oven; press a chocolate star or kiss in center.

# FROSTED MOLASSES CREAMS

| | |
|---|---|
| 1/2 c. shortening | 1/2 tsp. salt |
| 1/2 c. sugar | 1 1/2 tsp. baking powder |
| 1 well-beaten egg | 1/4 tsp. soda |
| 1/2 c. light molasses | 1 tsp. instant coffee |
| 1/2 c. hot water | 1 tsp. cinnamon |
| 1 1/2 c. sifted enriched flour | 1/2 tsp. cloves |

Thoroughly cream shortening and sugar; add egg and molasses; mix well. Add hot water. Sift dry ingredients; add to creamed mixture; beat until smooth. Pour into greased 13x9 1/2x2-inch pan. Bake in moderate oven (350°) 25 minutes. While warm, frost with confectioners' icing. Cool and cut in squares. Makes 1 1/2 dozen.

# CHOCOLATE CHEESECAKE BROWNIES

### Mix and pat into a 9x13-inch pan:
| | |
|---|---|
| 1 German chocolate cake mix | 1/2 c. coconut |
| 1/3 c. margarine, melted | 1 egg |

### Beat and spread on bottom layer:
| | |
|---|---|
| 2 eggs | 3/4 c. sugar |
| 2 8-oz. cream cheese | 2 tsp. vanilla |

Bake at 350° for 20-25 minutes. Cool and spread with topping.

## TOPPING:

**Mix:** 2 c. sour cream
1/4 c. sugar
1 tsp. vanilla

**Spread on top of cooled brownies and refrigerate.**

# THREE-LAYER BARS

Club crackers
2/3 c. sugar
1/2 c. brown sugar
1 c. crushed graham
  crackers

1/4 c. milk
1 stick margarine
2/3 c. peanut butter
1/2 c. chocolate chips
1/2 c. butterscotch chips

Line a lightly greased 9x13-inch pan with whole club crackers. Heat sugars, graham cracker crumbs, milk, and margarine to a slow boil. Pour over crackers in pan; add another layer of club crackers. Melt together peanut butter and both kinds of chips. Pour over crackers; cool.

# ALMOND SHORTBREAD
# SHAMROCK COOKIES

1 c. (2 sticks) butter, room temperature
7-oz. package almond paste, grated
1/2 c. sugar
1/4 tsp. vanilla extract
2 c. flour
2 T. milk (opt.)
Green sugar sprinkles (opt.)

With an electric mixer, beat butter on high for 3 min. or until very soft and light in color. Add grated almond

paste and sugar. Mix on low speed until combined.
Turn mixer to high; beat a full 5 min. or more, until
almost white-colored and fluffy. Mix in vanilla. Gently
stir flour into mixture until just combined. Spoon 1/2 of
dough onto a 50-inch-long piece of wax paper. With
hands, press dough out to a 1/4-inch thickness. Top
with wax paper. Lightly smooth top with rolling pin.
Keeping wax paper in place, lay dough on cookie sheet.
Repeat with remaining dough; chill 1 hour till firm.

Preheat oven to 325°. Line cookie sheets with parchment or foil. Work with one piece of dough at a time, keeping other half refrigerated. Cut out cookie shapes, shamrocks or as desired, and place on cookie sheets 2-inches apart, dipping cutters in flour if sticking. Repeat until all dough is used. Keep unbaked cookies refrigerated until ready to bake. Bake plain or brush tops with milk and sprinkle with green sugar. Bake for 12-14 min. or until cookies are firm and bottoms are very light golden. Cool on wire racks. Makes about 4 dozen.

# CANDIES

# CHOCOLATE FOR CANDY DIPPING

1/4 stick paraffin
1 large pkg. semi-sweet chocolate chips -
       can use milk chocolate, but candy too
       sweet for most tastes.
Melt in pan over very low heat. Stir lots. Or melt in
double boiler.
This chocolate is used for dipping peanut butter cups
and turtles. Add salted Spanish peanuts to left-over
chocolate. Drop by teaspoon on lightly greased cookie
sheets for peanut clusters.

# PEANUT BUTTER CUPS

| | |
|---|---|
| 1 stick butter (margarine) | 2 c. peanut butter |
| 3 c. powdered sugar | 1/2 tsp. vanilla |

Mix all ingredients together. Roll into small balls. Place on lightly-greased cookie sheets and chill. Dip chilled peanut butter balls in chocolate. Set back on cookie sheet. Chill again.

# TURTLES

Grease cookie sheet. Place on it 3 pecan halves for each turtle. Caramel - Use either method 1 or method 2.

1. Put 1 caramel on pecans. Heat in 350° oven until caramel is soft; flatten. Cool; dip in chocolate.

2. Home-made Caramels:

| | |
|---|---|
| 2 c. brown sugar | 1/2 c. butter |
| 1 c. white syrup | 1/2 tsp. salt |
| 1 1/2 c. evaporated milk | 1 tsp. vanilla |

Combine everything but vanilla in big <u>heavy</u> pan. Heat very slowly to boil until soft-ball stage. Scorches easily. Cook slowly. Stir often after it begins to boil. Remove from heat. Add vanilla. Drop spoonful on pecans; cool. Dip in chocolate.

# CHOCOLATE-COCONUT CREAMS

3/4 c. mashed potatoes
1 lb. (4 c.) flaked coconut
1 lb. (4 c.) sifted confectioners' sugar
1 tsp. almond extract
18-oz. semi-sweet chocolate chips

Combine first four ingredients in bowl with electric mixer. Blend well. Drop by heaping teaspoon on waxed paper. Roll in balls. Chill for 1 - 1 1/2 hours. Melt chocolate chips and around 1/8 stick of paraffin together. Dip each ball in chocolate mixture. Place on wax paper to harden. Makes 50-60 candies.

# PECAN CLUSTERS

3 (6-oz.) pkg. chocolate chips
1 pt. marshmallow cream
1 can sweetened condensed milk
2 1/2 - 3 c. pecans

Melt chocolate chips. Stir in condensed milk and marsh-mallow cream. Add pecans. Drop by teaspoonful on buttered pans.

# FILBERT FANCIES

1 c. shelled, un-
    blanched filberts
1 beaten egg
2 c. sifted powdered
    sugar
3 T. margarine, or
    butter, softened
1 tsp. vanilla

Dash of salt
2 (1-oz.) squares un-
    sweetened chocolate,
    melted and cooled
1 (6-oz.) pkg. miniature
    marshmallows
1 c. shredded coconut

Coarsely chop filberts; spread on baking sheet. Toast at 350°F until golden brown, about 10 minutes. Cool.

Combine egg, sugar, butter, vanilla, and dash of salt. Beat until very light and fluffy. Blend in chocolate. Combine marshmallows and filberts; fold in chocolate mixture. Drop from teaspoon into bowl of coconut; roll evenly to coat. Place on waxed paper-lined baking sheet. Let stand until set. Makes 4 dozen.

# MARSHMALLOW FUDGE

| | |
|---|---|
| 1/2 c. margarine | 2/3 c. evaporated milk |
| 1 1/2 c. sugar | 3 c. chocolate chips |

Mix in heavy saucepan. Bring to a full boil, stirring constantly. Continue boiling 5 min. over med. heat or until candy thermometer reaches 234°F, stirring constantly to prevent scorching. Remove from heat. Gradually stir in chocolate chips until melted. Add these ingredients: 7 oz. jar marshmallow creme, 1 c. chopped nuts and 1 tsp. vanilla. Mix well. Pour into greased 9-inch pan. Chill at room temperature.

# TWO-FLAVOR FUDGE

| | |
|---|---|
| 2 c. brown sugar | 1 c. canned milk |
| 1 c. sugar | 1/2 c. butter |

Boil 15 minutes over moderate heat. Stir occasionally.
Remove from heat.

**Add:**

1 (5-10 oz.) jar marshmallow cream

1 pkg. butterscotch chips     1 pkg. chocolate chips

Stir until melted.

**Add:**

| | |
|---|---|
| 1 c. nuts | 1 tsp. vanilla |

Pour into greased 9 x 13-inch pan and let set up.

# MICROWAVE FUDGE

2 1/4 c. sugar
2/3 c. evaporated milk
1/2 c. margarine
1 (7-oz.) jar marshmallow
    creme
1 (6-oz.) pkg. semi-sweet
    chocolate chips

1 (1-oz.) square un-
    sweetened baking
    chocolate
1/2 c. chopped nuts
    (pecans or walnuts)

Put sugar, milk, margarine, and marshmallow creme in
2-quart glass bowl. Microwave on high 3 min.; stir well.

Continue to microwave when it boils. Reduce to 50%, or medium; boil 5 min. Reduce power if it starts boiling over. Should be light almond color. Add chocolate chips and chocolate square; stir until melted. Fold in nuts and put in buttered 8-inch square pan. Cool several hours before cutting in squares. Makes 2 lbs.

# HOMEMADE CARAMELS

| | |
|---|---|
| 1 1/4 c. dark corn syrup | 1 c. butter |
| 2 c. sugar | 1 tsp. vanilla |
| 2 c. rich cream (whipping cream) | Nuts, optional |

Put syrup, sugar, 1 c. cream, and butter on heat. Stir; cook until mixture is boiling vigorously. Then stir in gradually the second cup of cream so boiling doesn't stop. Cook until a hard ball forms in cold water (30 to 40 min.). Add vanilla; beat well by hand. (Setting pan in cold water helps it harden.) Add nuts; pour into a buttered pan. When nearly cold, cut into squares and wrap in waxed paper.

# FRUIT AND NUT ALMOND BARK

1 (1 1/2 lb.) pkg.
  almond bark
2 c. raisins

2 c. English walnuts,
  chopped
1 (12-oz.) pkg. Chinese
  noodles

Melt almond bark in a double boiler or in microwave. Have ready in a large bowl, the raisins, walnuts, and Chinese noodles. Mix this together carefully; pour the melted bark over this; mix carefully. Drop by spoonful onto waxed paper. Let cool. Makes 45 clusters.

# TOFFEE

| | |
|---|---|
| 1 c. butter | 1 T. white corn syrup |
| 1 c. sugar | 3/4 c. chopped nuts (opt.) |
| 2 T. water | 6 to 8 oz. pkg. chocolate chips |

Melt butter on low heat in heavy saucepan. Remove from heat. Add sugar; mix together. Return to low heat; stir until mixture comes to a full rolling boil. Add water and syrup; stir. Cook until soft-crack stage (hard thread in cold water) 290°. Remove from heat. Add 1/4 c. nuts.

Pour into lightly buttered 13x9 cake pan; spread evenly.
When cool, spread with melted chocolate chips.
Sprinkle with rest of finely chopped nuts. Remove from
pan and break into serving pieces.

# PEANUT BRITTLE

Boil 1/2 c. water in heavy large pan; add 2 c. sugar and
1 c. white syrup. Stir until dissolved; boil until spins
long thread (240°) when dropped from spoon.
**Add:**
2 c. or 1 sack raw peanuts. Stir and cook until syrup
turn slightly golden and you can smell peanuts cooking
(290°). Don't cook until brown, but don't undercook or
candy will be chewy not brittle.

Remove from fire. Add 2 T. butter and 1 tsp. vanilla. Stir. Have 2 tsp. soda measured out; stir in last. Stir just until soda is mixed. Work quickly. Drop on buttered cookie sheets. Don't spread with spatula or spoon. Spreading will break air bubbles - the more air bubbles the better the peanut brittle. It will run and spread itself. Put pan in cold area quickly; pan gets very hot fast. When cold, break into serving pieces.

# DIVINITY

2 1/2 c. sugar
1/2 c. corn syrup
1/2 c. boiling water
2 drops lemon flavoring

2 egg whites
1 c. nuts
1 tsp. vanilla
Food coloring

Boil sugar, syrup and water. Beat egg whites until stiff. When syrup mixture threads, beat 1/2 c. syrup mixture into egg whites. Beat constantly. When rest of syrup mixture cracks in cold water, add to egg white and syrup mixture. Beat until it sets. Add nuts and lemon flavoring. If desired, add red or green food coloring.

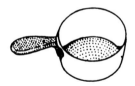

# BONBON CANDIES

## CANDY:

1 (3-oz.) pkg. cream cheese    1 tsp. vanilla
4 c. powdered sugar    1/2 c. black walnuts
1/3 c. cocoa

Bring cream cheese to room temperature. Use mixer to blend candy ingredients. Roll in little balls. Then chill completely. Then dip into coating.

## COATING:

2 T., or more, margarine   1 (6-oz.) pkg. p. butter chips
Melt margarine and peanut butter chips.  Put each ball
on a pickle fork, one at a time; dip into melted mixture
until all covered.  Put on waxed paper; refrigerate.

# TWIN-FLAVOR CLUSTERS

1 6-oz. pkg. butterscotch morsels
1 6-oz. pkg. chocolate morsels
1 can shoestring potatoes
1/2 small can peanuts or 1 1/2 cup

Melt butterscotch and chocolate morsels in double boiler. Add shoestring potatoes and peanuts. Spoon out to cool on wax paper. Leave pan over hot water while spooning out.

# MINTS

8-oz. pkg. cream cheese
2 lb. bag powdered sugar
Mint extract
Food coloring (pink, blue, yellow, etc.)

Mix softened cream cheese and powdered sugar. Add a
cap or more of mint extract; mix. Then separate into
however many colors you wish. Add as much food
coloring as desired to each batch. Mix; then press into a
mold or roll into a ball. Flatten, let dry. Eat or freeze.

# ROCKY ROAD CANDY

In top of double boiler, melt:
>    12 oz. pkg. chocolate chips
>    1 can Eagles Brand milk (14.5-oz.)
>    2 T. butter

Mix in very large bowl:
>    10.5-oz. pkg. miniature marshmallows
>    2 c. dry roasted peanuts

Pour chocolate mixture over mixture in bowl. Then pour on wax paper in 13x9x2 pan and chill for 2 hours or until firm. Peel wax paper off, cut and store in covered container.

# NEED GIFTS?

Are you up a stump for some nice gifts for some nice people in your life? Here's a list of some great cookbooks. Just check 'em off, stick a check in an envelope with these pages, and we'll get your books off to you. Add $3.50 for shipping and handling for the first book and then $.50 cents more for each additional one. If you order over $50.00, forget the shipping and handling.

## $5.95 Mini Cookbooks
### (Only 3 1/2 x 5) With Maxi Good Eatin' - 160 or 176 pages - $5.95

- ❑ Alabama Cooking
- ❑ Arkansas Cooking
- ❑ Dixie Cooking
- ❑ Georgia Cooking
- ❑ Illinois Cooking
- ❑ Indiana Cooking
- ❑ Iowa Cookin'
- ❑ Kansas Cookin'
- ❑ Massachusetts Cooking
- ❑ Minnesota Cookin'
- ❑ Missouri Cookin'
- ❑ New Hampshire Cooking
- ❑ New Jersey Cooking
- ❑ New York Cooking
- ❑ North Carolina Cooking
- ❑ Off To College Cookbook
- ❑ Ohio Cooking
- ❑ Pennsylvania Cooking
- ❑ South Carolina Cooking
- ❑ Tennessee Cooking
- ❑ Virginia Cooking
- ❑ Wisconsin Cooking

- ❑ Blueberry Blues Cookbook
- ❑ Citrus! Citrus! Citrus!
- ❑ Cooking Seafood & Poultry w/Wine
- ❑ Cooking with Asparagus
- ❑ Cooking with Cider
- ❑ Cooking with Garlic
- ❑ Cooking with Spirits
- ❑ Cooking with Sweet Onions
- ❑ Cooking with Wine
- ❑ Cooking with Things Go Baa
- ❑ Cooking with Things Go Cluck
- ❑ Cooking with Things Go Moo
- ❑ Cooking with Things Go Oink
- ❑ Cooking with Things Go Splash
- ❑ CSA Cookbook ($4.95)
- ❑ Crazy for Basil
- ❑ Dixie Cookbook
- ❑ Good Cookin' From the Plain People
- ❑ Great New England Cookbook
- ❑ Kid Money
- ❑ Kid Pumpkin Fun Book
- ❑ Midwest Small Town Cookin'

- ❑ Muffins Cookbook (Veggies, Fruit, Nut)
- ❑ Nuts! Nuts! Nuts!
- ❑ Recipes for Appetizers & Beverages Using Wine
- ❑ Recipes for Desserts Using Wine
- ❑ Super Simple Cookin'
- ❑ To Take the *Gamey* out of the Game
- ❑ Working Girl Cookbook

## $6.95 Mini Cookbooks
### 176 - 204 pages - $6.95

- ❑ Arizona Cooking
- ❑ Bountiful Blueberries
- ❑ Dakota Cooking
- ❑ Kentucky Cookin'
- ❑ Southwest Cooking
- ❑ Amish-Mennonite Apple Cookbook
- ❑ Amish-Mennonite Berry Cookbook
- ❑ Amish-Mennonite Peach Cookbook
- ❑ Amish-Mennonite Pumpkin Cookbook
- ❑ Amish & Mennonite Strawberry Cookbook

## ($6.95 continued)

- Apples Galore
- Apples! Apples! Apples!
- Berries! Berries! Berries!
- Berries Galore
- Cherries Galore
- Cooking Greens Southern Style
- Cooking with Mulling Spices
- Crockpot Cookbook
- Grass-Fed Beef Recipes
- The Grilling & BBQ Cookbook
- Holiday & Get-Together Cookbook
- Herbs! Herbs! Herbs!
- How to Make Salsa
- Kid Cookin'
- New Mexico Cooking
- Peaches! Peaches! Peaches!
- Pecans! Pecans! Pecans!
- Pumpkins! Pumpkins! Pumpkins!
- Renaissance Cokery Boke
- Some Like It Hot
- Soup's On!
- Veggie Talk Coloring & Story Book
- Winter Squash Cookbook
- The Zero Calorie Chocolate Cookbook

## In-Between Cookbooks
**(5 1/2 x 8 1/2) - 150 pages - $9.95**

- Adaptable Apple Cookbook
- Amish Ladies Cookbook - Old Husbands
- Amish Ladies Cookbook - Young Husbands
- Amish Ladies Carry-To-The-Field Cold Lunches Cookbook
- An Apple A Day Cookbook
- Baseball Moms' Cookbook
- Basketball Moms' Cookbook
- Bird Up! Pheasant Cookbook
- Buffalo Cookbook
- Camp Cookin'
- Catfish Cookin' Cookbook
- Civil War Cookin', Stories, 'n Such
- Cherokee Native American Book of Recipes
- Cooking Ala Nude
- Cooking for a Crowd
- Cooking Up Some Winners Cookbook
- Cooking with Beer
- Cooking with Moonshine
- Cooking with Sorghum
- Country Cooking Amish Heritage
- Das Hausbarn Cookbook

- Eating Ohio
- Eat Cheap Cookbook
- Farmers Market Cookbook
- Feast of Moons Indian Cookbook
- Funky Duck Cookbook
- Halloween Fun Book
- Hunting in the Nude Cookbook
- Indian Cooking Cookbook
- Japanese Cooking
- Keep The Skinny Kid Skinny
- Kids' No-Cook Cookbook
- Mad About Garlic
- Market to Kitchen
- Mormon Trail Cookbook
- New Cooks' Cookbook
- No-Stove, No-Sharp Knife Kids'
- Norwegian Cooking
- Off the Farm, Out of the Garden
- Outdoor Cooking for Outdoor Men
- Plantation Cookin' Cookbook
- Pumpkin Patch, Proverbs & Pies
- Shhh Cookbook
- Soccer Mom's Cookbook
- SW Native American Cookbook
- Southwest Vegetarian Cookbook
- Trailer Trash Cookbook
- Vegan Vegetarian Cookbook
- Venison Cookbook